WINNERS ON THE ICE

Winners on the Ice

BY FRANK LITSKY

A PICTURE LIFE BOOK
FRANKLIN WATTS
NEW YORK | LONDON | 1979

FRONTISPIECE:
JOHN CURRY WORKING OUT.

Library of Congress Cataloging in Publication Data

Litsky, Frank.
Winners on the ice.

(A Picture life book)
SUMMARY: Biographical sketches of eight ath-
letes who worked to become skating champions.

1. Skaters—Biography—Juvenile literature. [1. Ice
skaters] I. Title.
GV850.A2L57   796.9'1'0922 [B] [920]   78-23454
ISBN 0-531-02291-9

Photographs courtesy of Chris Little: frontispiece;
Skating Magazine: opp. p. 1, pp. 7, 8 (Elissa Bald-
win), 15 (Roger F. Turner Jr.), and 26; *The New
York Times:* pp. 3 (Paul Hosefros), 4, 12, 19, 25, 30,
and 34 (Joe Traver); Steven E. Sutton/Duomo:
p. 11; United Press International: p. 16; All-Sport/
Duomo: p. 20; Francis Ing: p. 29; Wide World
Photos: pp. 37, 39, and 40 (left and right).

Cover photo of Dorothy Hamill by George Kalinsky.
Cover photo of Charles Tickner
by Steven E. Sutton/Duomo.
Cover photo of Sheila Young
by Duomo/All-Sport

R.L. 2.3 Spache Revised Formula

CONTENTS

Dorothy showing off one of her first trophies.

DOROTHY HAMILL

The American skater Dorothy Hamill was born in 1956 in Riverside, Connecticut. When she was 8 years old, she got a pair of skates for Christmas. She started skating on a frozen pond near her home. Before long, she asked for lessons.

By 14 years old, Dorothy knew she wanted to be a champion skater. But she had a problem. She didn't have enough time to train. She discussed it with her family. They took her out of school. She studied at home with a private teacher. This allowed her the time she needed.

At 17, Dorothy's life changed again. She moved to Colorado. There she began training with a famous coach. His name was Carlo Fassi. She trained seven hours a day. She trained six days a week. And she trained 11 months a year.

In 1974, Dorothy became United States champion. In 1975 and 1976, she won the same title again. Then, later in 1976, she won the biggest title of all. She became an Olympic champion.

The Winter Olympics were in Austria that year. Each figure skater skated on three separate days. The first two days everyone had to follow a set routine. The third day was for free skating. The skaters would skate their own routines.

Dorothy and her mother at Riverside School in Connecticut. The stuffed toy refers to a skating figure Dorothy did at the Olympics, known as the Hamill camel.

Dorothy did very well the first two days. But on the third day, she was great. For four straight minutes she dazzled the crowd. She leaped and spun and jumped.

The best possible score the judges could give was a 6.0. This is a perfect score. Dorothy was almost perfect. Her scores were all 5.8s and 5.9s. They earned her a gold medal.

After the Olympics, Dorothy won the world championship. Then she joined the Ice Capades. This is an ice show. She has skated all over the United States and Canada.

Figure skating is fun to watch. No one has made it more fun than Dorothy Hamill.

Dorothy performing in the Ice Capades in 1977.

CHARLES TICKNER

Ice skaters are graceful. But sometimes they fall. Charles Tickner has fallen a lot. Something always seemed to go wrong when he skated. But he still became a world figure-skating champion.

Charles was born in 1953 in Oakland, California. He started to skate when he was 9. At first, he was terrible. He was good at other sports. But he couldn't skate at all. That bothered him. So he kept at it until he learned. But he didn't really want to be a great skater.

Charles at the age of 9.

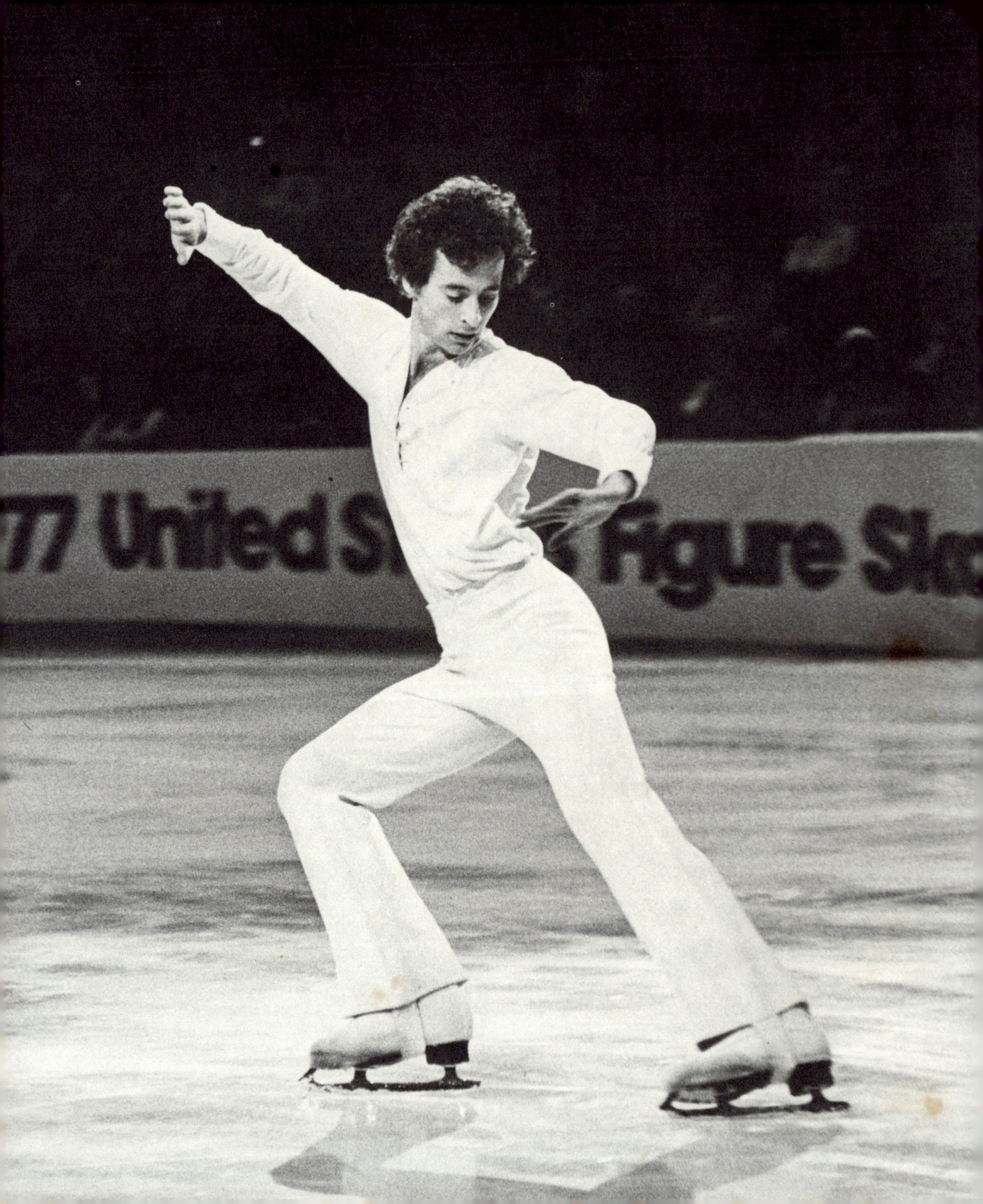
77 United
Figure

Then, when he was 19 years old, he moved to Littleton, Colorado. He started training there with a new coach. The coach's name was Norma Sahlin. Charles lived with Norma and her husband. He started to train seven hours a day.

He was a good student. He made skating look easy. But he was always afraid of making mistakes. He wanted to quit.

Norma didn't know what to do. Finally, she got an idea. She told Charles to talk to himself. At the beginning of each session he should say things like, "Relax, Charles, relax. You can do it. You can win."

Charles took Norma's advice. It helped. But he still had problems.

In 1974, during the U.S. championships, he fell twice. In 1976, he fell twice again. He couldn't make the Olympic team.

Charles winning his first
national title in 1977.

Then things got better. In 1977, he won the U.S. championship. He won it again in 1978. Later in 1978, he went to the world championships. Nobody thought he would win. Not even Charles. He would have been glad to finish second or third.

At the end of the first day, he was in third place. At the end of the second day, he moved into second. On the third and last day, he was superb. He made four triple jumps. This brought the crowd to its feet. These are the hardest jumps to do. When he finished, the crowd stood and cheered. They knew he had won. He was the new world champion.

This is part of the free skating routine that won Charles the world championship in 1978.

PEGGY FLEMING

To be a good figure skater, you must be strong. You must also be graceful. Peggy Fleming became famous for being graceful. She skates like a ballet dancer. Watching her skate is almost like a dream.

Peggy was born in 1948 in San Jose, California. Her father was in the newspaper business. When Peggy was growing up, her father changed jobs often. So the family moved around a lot.

Peggy competing at 15.

Peggy started skating when she was 9. At 11 she began competing. When she was 15, she won her first United States championship. That was in 1964. Then she went to the Winter Olympics in Austria. She finished sixth.

After this, the Fleming family moved to Colorado. They moved there so Peggy could be coached by Carlo Fassi. She went to high school there with many other skaters. The school knew she needed time to skate. It helped her find the time.

Peggy just after winning her first U.S. championship title.

She got up at five o'clock every morning. She skated from six o'clock to eleven o'clock. Then she went to classes. She skated again from five in the afternoon to eight at night. After this, she would study.

Peggy won the U.S. championship five years in a row — from 1964 to 1968. She won the world championship three years in a row — from 1966 to 1968. But what she wanted most was an Olympic gold medal. In 1968, in France, she got it.

After the Olympics, Peggy became a professional skater. She skated with the Ice Follies. She has appeared often on television. Dorothy Hamill may have brought fun to figure skating. Peggy Fleming brought beauty.

Peggy performing at
Madison Square Garden in 1974.

IRINA RODNINA

Most figure skaters skate alone. During
competition, only one skater skates at a
time. That kind of skating is called singles.
But there are two other kinds of figure
skating. One is called pairs. The other
is called dancing. In these, a man and a
woman skate together.

The best pairs skater in the world is
a woman from the Soviet Union. Her
name is Irina Rodnina (EAR-in-na
ROAD-nin-uh). Irina was born in Moscow
in 1949. Her father is an Army officer.
Her mother works in an office.

Irina with Alexei Ulanov, her first partner.
They are practicing here for the 1969
world championship competition.

Irina doing a "death spiral" with
her second partner, husband
Alexandr Zaitsev, in the 1976 Olympics.

Irina is a shy, quiet person. But when she skates, she is exciting. She even gets excited herself.

Irina started competing when she was 15. Her first coach was Stanislav Zhuk. He was very hard on her. Sometimes she didn't like him at all.

Irina's first pairs partner was Alexei Ulanov. Together they won four world championships in a row, starting in 1969. They won the Olympic gold medal in 1972. Then Alexei fell in love with another skater and married her. Irina lost her partner.

Her new partner was Alexandr Zaitsev. Alexandr was a good skater, but Irina was worried. She had never won a competition without Alexei. She had a bad fall before one event. She won the event anyway, but it still made her afraid.

Fortunately, nothing like that happened again. Alexandr and Irina won every time they skated. They won the world championship every year starting in 1973. In 1975, they were married. They won the Olympic gold medal in 1976. In 1978, Irina won the world championship for her tenth year in a row.

Irina and Alexandr live and train in Leningrad. Both go to a sports school there. They like to go to the theatre and ballet. They also like to dance. Irina says she will continue skating as long as she enjoys it. And as long as people enjoy watching her.

DICK BUTTON

Years ago, figure skating was different. There were jumps and spins, as there are now. But most figure skaters just didn't train that hard.

One American skater changed all that. His name was Dick Button.

Dick was born in 1929 in Englewood, New Jersey. When he was 11, he got skates for Christmas. They were hockey skates, though. Dick returned them to the store. He got figure skates instead.

Dick didn't look like a figure skater. He was fat and clumsy. At 12, he asked for lessons. His first teacher said, "He'll never make a skater. Never. Not in a million years. He's too fat."

His parents found another coach. When Dick was 13, he entered his first contest. He finished second.

Dick loved skating. He was a real athlete. In winter, he would take his skates to school. He would even wear skating clothes to class. That way, he'd have more time for skating after school. His teachers didn't like that. They told him to dress more appropriately.

Dick started training hard. He got up at 5:30 every morning. He skated five or six hours a day. He got taller and thinner.

At 14, he won the U.S. novice championship. At 15, he won the U.S. junior championship. At 16, he won the

U.S. men's championship. He became the youngest skater ever to win that title. In fact, he won it seven years in a row— from 1946 to 1952. He also won the world championship five times. And he won Olympic gold medals in 1948 and 1952. He was the first American to win an Olympic figure skating title.

Dick, who has just returned from the 1948 Olympics, is being welcomed home by his parents.

After graduating from college, Dick joined the Ice Capades. He skated all over America. Later, he started his own ice show.

Now, Dick is a lawyer and businessman. He thinks up ideas for television shows. You may have seen one of his shows. It is called *Superstars*. Dick is also a commentator on televised skating events. He tells listeners what the skaters are doing.

Dick changed the style
of men's figure skating
with athletic leaps
such as this one.

JOHN CURRY

John Curry wanted to be a dancer.
Instead, he became a figure skater. But
he skates like a ballet dancer. And he
became the best figure skater in the
world.

John was born in 1949 in Birmingham,
England. When he was 6 years old, he
saw ballet dancing on television. He liked
it. He asked for dance lessons. His father
said no.

That same year, John saw figure
skating on television. He liked that, too.
His mother took him skating. He loved it.

John exhibiting
the gold medal
he won at the
1976 Olympics.

Jumps such as this one
were very difficult
for John to master.

The first day, he skated a short distance. He held the barrier with one hand. The skating teacher held his other hand. John told the teacher to let go. "I'll do it by myself," he said. And he did.

A few months later, John competed for the first time. He won first place.

John kept winning, but he had some problems. He didn't like jumping. Once, he fell six times in three minutes. Another time, he skated off the ice in the middle of his routine.

In 1972, John came in fourth in the world championship. But he wasn't happy with that. He knew he needed good coaching. He didn't have the money for it. He was ready to stop skating.

Then a lucky thing happened. A wealthy American saw John skate and offered to help. He gave John money to go to the United States.

There, John trained with two coaches. The coaches taught him jumping. They made him work hard. Every day, John would do figure eights for three hours. Then he would free skate for three hours. Often, he'd follow this with a dance lesson for an hour. Two nights a week, he worked with weights.

In 1976, John became a winner. First, he won the European championship. Then he entered the Olympics. He was behind the leader until the last day. On the last day he did his free skating routine. A perfect score is 6.0. Almost every judge gave John a score of 5.9. He won the gold medal. Later in that year, he won the world championship.

That was John's last competition. After that, he turned professional. He formed his own skating troupe.

ERIC HEIDEN

There are three different sports that use skates. One is figure skating. One is hockey. Hockey is played by teams. The third is speed skating. There are no tricks, jumps, or spins in speed skating. All you try to do is skate fast.

The most famous speed skater in the world today is an American, Eric Heiden (HIGH-den). Eric comes from Madison, Wisconsin. He was born in 1958. Eric's father, a doctor, used to play hockey. Eric's mother was a swimmer. Eric's grandfather was a hockey coach.

Eric (right) begins to pass Johan Granath
of Sweden in the 1,000-m race at the
1978 world speed skating championships.
Eric won the race and the title.

When Eric was only 2, he got his first skates. His father took him to a frozen lake near home. Eric tried to skate. But he kept falling down. He told his father, "I'm too little to skate." His father said, "Okay. We'll come back next week."

When Eric was 5, he tried figure skating. When he was 8, he tried speed skating. He liked speed skating better. He liked to race against other boys.

In high school, Eric played hockey and soccer. When he was 14, though, he broke a tooth during a hockey game. His mother tried to get him to stop playing hockey. She encouraged him to speed skate instead. She felt it was safer. He agreed.

In 1976, Eric made the U.S. Olympic team. He skated in two Olympic races. He finished seventh in one and nineteenth in the other.

Then, in 1977, something extraordinary happened. There were three world championships in three weeks. They were all held in Europe. The first one was for the overall championship. An American had never won it. Eric won it. The next was the junior championship. Eric won that, too. The last was the sprint championship. No American man had ever won that either. Eric won it. Eric became the first skater ever to win the three championships in one year.

Afterward, Eric returned from Europe and went to college. He attended the University of Wisconsin. For one month, he rested. Then he started training again. He'd drive 75 miles (121 km) a day to skate at an outdoor rink.

In 1978, Eric skated in the three world championships again. Again he won all three.

Eric's younger sister, Beth, is a skater, too. In 1978, Beth won the world junior championship. She almost won the sprint championship also.

There are only 5,000 speed skaters in the United States. There are many more in Europe. But Eric Heiden is the best in the world. Eric is proud of that. He has always worked hard. Now it is paying off.

Eric and his younger sister Beth, both world champions.

SHEILA YOUNG

Sheila Young wanted to be a good speed
skater. So she raced bicycles to get
stronger. She became so good on her
bike that she won two world bicycle
championships. She also won world
championships in speed skating. She
broke several world speed-skating records.
And in 1976, she did something no
American had ever done before.

Sheila (left), even at the age of 9,
shows style and determination
as she skates here with the
Wolverine Sports Club in Detroit.

Left: Sheila winning
the 500-m race at the
1973 world speed
skating championships
in Oslo, Norway.
Right: Sheila winning
the 1976 world
cycling championships.

Sheila was born in 1950 in Birmingham, Michigan. Her father had once been a speed skater. Her mother had once been a bicycle champion. Sheila started skating when she was 9. She learned quickly. When she was 13, she came in second in the U.S. championships.

At the age of 19, Sheila became a national skating champion. At 21, she became a national bicycle champion.

She liked speed skating better. But riding bikes helped her skate. They made her legs stronger.

Sheila trained for four hours a day. In the cold weather, she skated. When it was warm, she ran, exercised, and rode her bike.

In 1972, Sheila made the U.S. Olympic skating team. She finished fourth in her race. She was disappointed and thought about quitting. But she didn't.

In 1976, she went to the Winter Olympics in Austria. She held the world record in the 500-m race. Everyone thought she would win that race. But they didn't know she had injured her foot.

Sheila's first race was the 1,500-m. She finished second, and won a silver medal. The next day was the 500-m race. She finished first, and won a gold medal. Then, on the third day, there was the 1,000-m race. She finished third and won the bronze medal. So, in three days, Sheila won three Olympic medals. No American skater had ever done this before.

That summer, Sheila won the world bicycle championship. Then she married Jim Ochowicz. Jim was also a speed skater and bike racer. They now have a baby named Katie. Sheila has retired from sports. But she intends to help out in the 1980 Winter Olympics.